The Good Farmer

BY ALYSSA KREKELBERG

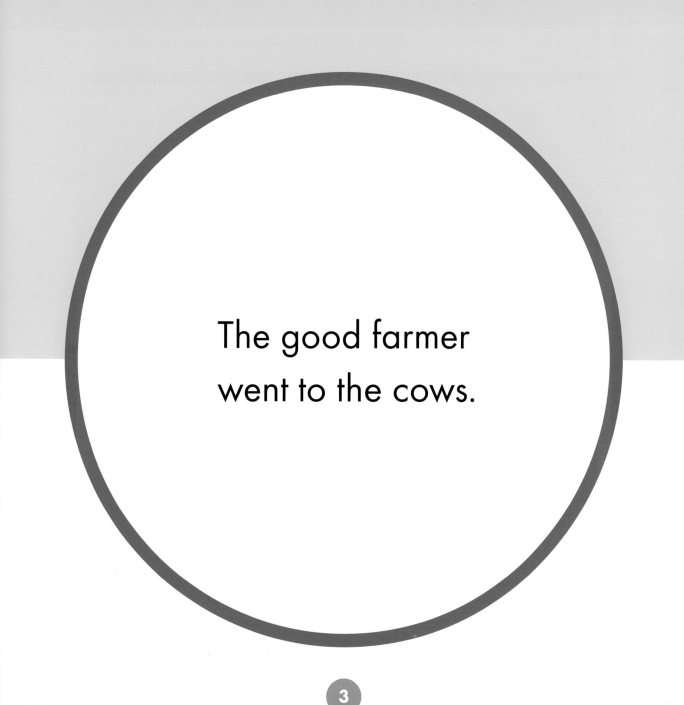

The good farmer
went to the cows.

The good farmer
must feed the cows.

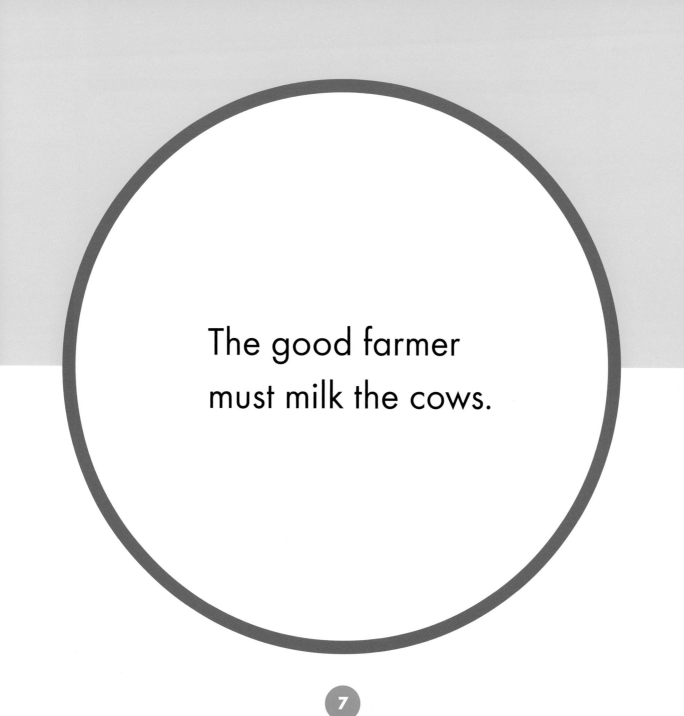

The good farmer
must milk the cows.

The good farmer
went to the horses.

The good farmer
must brush the horses.

The good farmer
went to the pigs.

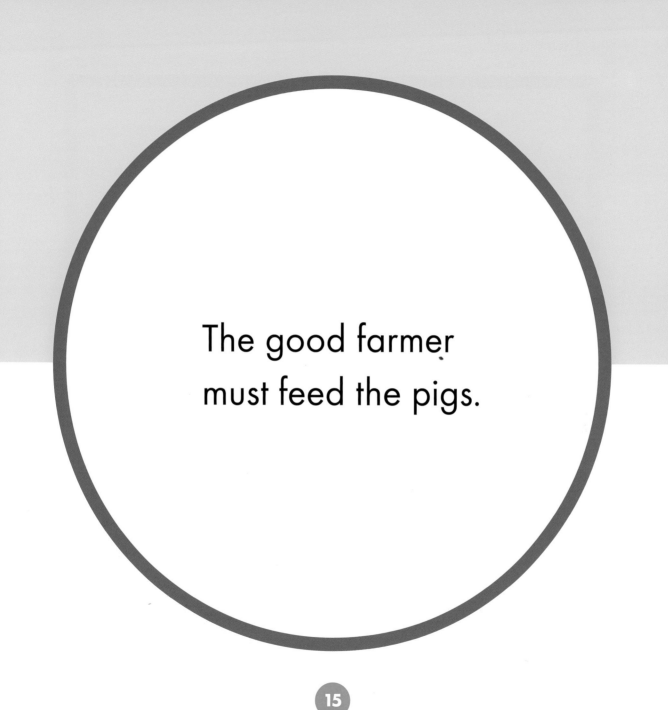

The good farmer
must feed the pigs.

The good farmer
went to the chickens.

The good farmer
must get the
chicken eggs.

The good farmer
must sit down.
He worked hard.

Note to Caregivers and Educators

Sight words are a foundation for reading. It's important for young readers to have sight words memorized at a glance without breaking them down into individual letter sounds. Sight words are often phonetically irregular and can't be sounded out, so readers need to memorize them. Knowing sight words allows readers to focus on more difficult words in the text. The intent of this book is to repeat specific sight words as many times as possible throughout the story. Through repetition of the words, emerging readers will recognize, and ideally memorize, each sight word. Memorizing sight words can help improve readers' literacy skills.

farmer

good

the

About the Author

Alyssa Krekelberg is a children's book editor and author. She lives in Minnesota and enjoys exploring the great outdoors with her hyper husky.

Published by The Child's World®
1980 Lookout Drive • Mankato, MN 56003-1705
800-599-READ • www.childsworld.com

Photographs ©: Diego Cervo/iStockphoto, cover, 1, 2, 5, 6, 21; iStockphoto, 9, 17, 18, 23; SCP Photography/Shutterstock Images, 10; Shutterstock Images, 13; Janis Susa/Shutterstock Images, 14

ISBN 9781503835603
LCCN 2019943119

Printed in the United States of America